WRITING DAYS

BOOKS BY JAN THOMPSON

CHRISTIAN BEACH ROMANCE & ROMANTIC WOMEN'S FICTION

Savannah Sweethearts (11 Books)
JanThompson.com/savannah

Vacation Sweethearts (5 Books)
JanThompson.com/vacation

Seaside Chapel (9-12 Books)
JanThompson.com/seaside

CHRISTIAN ROMANTIC SUSPENSE & INSPIRATIONAL THRILLERS

Protector Sweethearts (6 Books)
JanThompson.com/protector

Suspense Sweethearts Collection (Box Set)
JanThompson.com/suspense

Binary Hackers (3 Books)
JanThompson.com/binary

ENDORSEMENTS

"At last, a devotional that reaches into a writer's heart and soul! Whether you're a new writer or a seasoned one, *Writing Days* is a gem of a resource offering inspiration, encouragement, and godly wisdom 52 weeks of the year."

— LAURA FRANTZ, CHRISTY AWARD-
WINNING AUTHOR

"Jan Thompson's book, *Writing Days: 52 Devotionals for the 52 Weeks in a Christian Writer's Year*, includes timely Scriptures and thoughtful insights writers will appreciate, along with practical action steps they can take each week to draw closer to the Lord as they move ahead on their writing journey.

These devotions offer encouragement and provide a weekly spiritual focus that will help writers honor the Lord and find rest and joy as they write for Him."

— CARRIE TURANSKY, AWARD-
WINNING AUTHOR

"When I am writing it is so easy to let everything else in my life slide—especially devotions. Thompson's encouraging book does a wonderful job of setting the tone for the week by focusing our mind and hearts on God. It's a valuable resource that belongs on every writer's Kindle!"

— TRACI TYNE HILTON, AUTHOR OF THE *MITZY NEUHAUS MYSTERY* SERIES AND *THE PLAIN JANE MYSTERIES*

WRITING DAYS

52 Devotionals for 52 Writing Weeks

JAN THOMPSON

Georgia
Press

WRITING DAYS: 52 DEVOTIONALS FOR 52 WRITING WEEKS (CHRISTIAN BIBLE STUDY BOOK 1)

First eBook Edition: August 2014
ISBN: 978-1-944188-00-9

First Paperback Edition: August 2019
ISBN: 978-1-944188-55-9

To my Lord and Savior, Jesus Christ,
who died on the cross to save me from my sins
and rose again from the grave
to give me eternal life in heaven.

For God so loved the world,
that He gave His only begotten Son,
that whosoever believeth in Him
should not perish,
but have everlasting life.
—John 3:16

CONTENTS

ABOUT WRITING DAYS

Dear Christian writers,

Do you spend time in God's Word on a regular basis?

Are you at peace with where you are in your writing career? Or are you struggling through your writing days? Are you rejoicing in the goodness of God? Or are you having a wish-it-were-better writing season?

Regardless of where you are in your personal and professional writing journey, whether you are a published or unpublished writer, this inspirational weekly devotional book is for you.

Written in a pocketbook format so you can read each entry on your smart phone or tablets or alongside your Bible in your personal devotions or Bible study, *Writing Days* has one goal: to encourage you, Christian writer, in your daily and weekly walk with God, hopefully strengthening your faith in the Lord Jesus Christ as you serve Him through the gift of writing.

Writing Days eBook
JanThompson.com/writing

Writing Days Paperback
JanThompson.com/writing-paperback

———

May your writing journey be abundant, fruitful, and pleasing to God!

INTRODUCTION

Fifteen years before I started my writer's blog, *A Cup of Chai with Jan Thompson*, and seventeen years before I published my first books, I began to pray and seek God's will for my writing career.

I had expected that my experiences in life would inform how I blog and write, but it had also worked out the other way around. As I wrote my blog articles during the last two years, I learned more about God, more about my own writing voice, and more about my place as an author and publisher in the book world.

In *Writing Days*, I hope to share with you the verses I have learned in the last seventeen years of my writing life, verses that are still fresh in my mind, those gentle reminders that I felt the Lord has worked into my own heart. I hope these scriptural passages and my personal notes will encourage you in your own writing journey. Each devotional entry is for the entire week, but the daily action plans are for your consideration during the week.

I pray that the fifty-two weeks of your writing year will be fruitful and bring glory to God.

In Christ,
Jan Thompson
www.janthompson.com
August 2014

WRITING DAYS

WEEK 1: A TIME TO REST

> Return unto thy rest, O my soul; for the Lord hath dealt bountifully with thee.

— PSALM 116:7

*W*riters, are you at rest?

I've seen at least one meme on social media saying that we writers are always working, whether we're plotting or writing or editing.

While that might be true when I'm in the middle of a project or when I'm trying to meet publication deadlines, I often think about these:

- Am I doing what God has called me to do?
- Or am I writing because the idea of fame and fortune sounds glamorous?

I believe that if I am in the will of God for my life, then what He leads me to do, which might be difficult at times, doesn't give me grief or despair. I will not be restless or stressed out about it.

Obviously, there are times when I might be doing the right thing the wrong way, but that fault is mine. It's not God's calling that is in error, but it could be my modus operandi that are called into question.

Am I working out God's will in my own ways that have not been vetted by God or contrary to His Word? Then I would have no assurance of His approval, no peace in my heart, and no rest for the duration of the project.

Am I balancing my strengths and weaknesses against the time I have to do God's will?

Or am I in such a hurry that I miss the story arc that He has in mind? In my haste, have I modified His will for my writing career by adding to my plate such plots and plans that He hasn't called me to do?

Am I working in the strengths He has given me, or am I seeking to do things for which I have no gift, no skill, no calling? Uh-oh. That could be bad news.

When I am in God's will for my life and my

writing career, I can expect to be at rest. I am not agitated, filled with angst and worries, or roiled with frayed nerves. I am resting in Christ. I am at peace.

WEEK 1 DAILY ACTION PLAN:

Ask God to show you how to rest in Christ.

MY PERSONAL NOTES

And Action Plan

WEEK 2: AN ORDERLY ARRAY

66 Let all things be done decently and in order.

— I CORINTHIANS 14:40

Since the letters to the Corinthians had been translated from ancient Greek, I looked up Strong's concordance to see the meaning of the words for "decently" and "order."

- *Euschémonós*, translated as "decently," means "becomingly, decorously, honestly, properly," giving the idea of "having good form."

- *Taxis*, translated as "order," conveys the notion of having a "regular arrangement" and an "orderly array."

When I was a full-time database programmer, I used arrays a lot, whether to index a set of fields or to manage tables of data. I had arrays. And arrays of arrays. There were many ways to program the same piece of software to meet the specifications. All the time, my programming job was to bring order out of chaos and make sure those bits and bytes were nestled in their proper arrangements in the databases.

In a similar way, while there are many avenues to creative writing, many methods to achieving the same goal of producing a publishable book, God's Word reminds me to do everything decently and in order. To me, it means that I would not:

- Rush to publish new and future books, opening myself to possible mistakes.
- Rail against God when things don't go my way.

And it means that I would:

1. Reverence God.

2. Respect His perfect timing to get things done.
3. Remember to pray every step of the way to get it done right.

WEEK 2 DAILY ACTION PLAN:

Get organized and stay organized.

MY PERSONAL NOTES

And Action Plan

WEEK 3: TRUSTWORTHY GOD

> Trust in the Lord with all thine heart; and lean not unto thine own understanding. In all thy ways acknowledge him, and he shall direct thy paths.

— PROVERBS 3:5-6

The Word of God is sharper than any two-edged sword.

The Word of God always rings true.

The Word of God never fails.

And the Word of God says that if I acknowledge Him in all my ways, He will direct my paths.

It's my resolution, then, to learn to trust God at all times, in all things, in all ways, regardless of year and time of year, of season and changes in season.

After all, seasons come and go. God alone never changes.

Proverbs 3:5-6 is interesting in that it provides the steps and progression for divine help:

1. "Trust in the Lord with all thine heart."
2. "Lean not unto thine own understanding."
3. "In all thy ways acknowledge him."
4. "He shall direct thy paths."

Unless I trust God with all my heart, I would fall back to trusting my own finite vision.

If I fall back on human understanding, I would be too proud to acknowledge the Hand of God and His Lordship over my life.

As a result, I wouldn't have God's perfect navigational skills applied to my life's paths.

If I want the end result of divine guidance for my writing career, then I should start by trusting God with all my heart.

WEEK 3 DAILY ACTION PLAN

Think of God first above all else.

MY PERSONAL NOTES

And Action Plan

WEEK 4: RAISONS D'ÊTRE

For where your treasure is, there will your heart be also.

— LUKE 12:34

There are many things that can take me away from my writing goals that can catch me unaware as I wander into a side garden—smelling roses, taking pictures, sitting awhile on a lovely bench.

There is always a time for that, but if I'm in a race, then I need to finish it.

As a Christian writer, I find that keeping my eyes

on God's purpose for my life helps me advance toward my writing goals.

In some of my writing projects, I would start out with a grand parade and fireworks, but then somewhere along the uphill climb when the hike is steep, and I don't have the privilege of Samwise Gamgee carrying me on his back, I start to become weary, tired, exhausted, and wonder what in the world I am doing as a writer.

That's when I pause and evaluate.

I find it necessary to examine what I've been doing and where I've been. I ask myself these questions:

- What is my purpose for being a writer?
- Does what I want to do match up with God's best plan for my life?
- If I have deviated from my purpose, what must I do to get back on track? Does it require my repentance before God, or affirmation that I'm on the right path?
- Do my daily plans and writing schedules take me closer to fulfilling God's purpose for my life, not only my writing career?
- What inconsequential activities must I forsake to prevent me from being distracted from my daily purpose? Is it social media?
- Am I spread too thin?
- Am I being careful to stick to my priorities?

- Are these priorities from God or from myself?
- Are these priorities properly appropriated so that I have a balanced schedule between family and writing?
- Have I prayed through all my decisions so they line up with God's will for my life?

WEEK 4 DAILY ACTION PLAN

Know your calling and don't deviate from it.

MY PERSONAL NOTES

And Action Plan

WEEK 5: TAKE HEART

> And Jesus said unto him, Go thy way; thy faith hath made thee whole. And immediately he received his sight, and followed Jesus in the way.

— MARK 10:52

*V*erse 46 of the same chapter says that the man was "blind Bartimaeus, the son of Timaeus." He "sat by the highway side begging."

> And when he heard that it was Jesus of Nazareth, he began to cry out, and say,

Jesus, thou son of David, have mercy on me.

— MARK 10:47

Even when the crowd told him to shut up, Bartimaeus persisted, calling out to Jesus until Jesus responded.

> And Jesus stood still, and commanded him to be called. And they call the blind man, saying unto him, Be of good comfort, rise; he calleth thee. And he, casting away his garment, rose, and came to Jesus. And Jesus answered and said unto him, What wilt thou that I should do unto thee? The blind man said unto him, Lord, that I might receive my sight. And Jesus said unto him, Go thy way; thy faith hath made thee whole. And immediately he received his sight, and followed Jesus in the way.

— MARK 10:49-52

What came first in the healing of Bartimaeus? Faith.

What came after Bartimaeus's faith was secure? Jesus restored his sight.

To me, it means that I must first have faith in God before I can see Him at work. I must first believe that He is the "author and finisher" of my faith (Hebrews 12:2) before I can experience the joy that comes from believing.

My focus on God corrects my vision, affects my visual perspective, and fixes my outlook.

WEEK 5 DAILY ACTION PLAN

Ask God to increase your faith in Him.

MY PERSONAL NOTES

And Action Plan

WEEK 6: REMAIN CALM

> He maketh the storm a calm, so that the waves thereof are still.

— PSALM 107:29

*N*o matter what happens in my life, I need to remember that God is still God. God, who never panics, who knows all things, solves all problems, allows what He allows for a reason.

It is well with my soul, no matter what happens. It is going to be okay.

In my writing life, I can stay calm and focused on writing what I want to write, and I can leave the future in the perfect hand of God, whatever "The End" results. For example, it doesn't matter how fast other authors write. I have my own pace. I can remain calm and keep my eyes on my own finish line.

Each of us writes differently. Regardless of what people say about there being no new plot under the sun, the truth still remains that God has created each of us in a unique way. None of us has the same DNA or fingerprints or soul like another. We are unique.

Embedded in that uniqueness is God's plan and purpose for our lives. Knowing that God is sovereign over my past, present, and future enables me to remain calm in Christ while He calms the winds and waves of my writing days.

WEEK 6 DAILY ACTION PLAN

Pray that God will give you a calm spirit and a quiet heart.

MY PERSONAL NOTES

And Action Plan

WEEK 7: FIRE IN MY BONES

“ Then I said, I will not make mention of him, nor speak any more in his name. But his word was in mine heart as a burning fire shut up in my bones, and I was weary with forbearing, and I could not stay.

— JEREMIAH 20:9

*I*t's hard to explain, but there's this fire in my bones that I cannot hold back. I must write. I must speak. I must share. I must publish.

It is my desire that God finds me faithful not only in my writing career but also in my daily life when I'm not writing. Thus, whether I'm teaching, training, loving, living, mothering, mentoring, cooking, cleaning, working, writing, or whatever I'm doing, it would be in my best interests to do them well. God, who sees all, sees my heart, my attitude, and my fervor in my daily life.

This week, I do not want to quench the Holy Spirit in my life, prevent Him from blessing me, or let sin stifle my creativity. This week, I surrender to the Lord the "words of my mouth and the meditation of my heart" (Psalm 19:14) so that my writing projects will be in line with the fire He has put in my bones so that I will:

- Mention Him.
- Speak His name.

WEEK 7 DAILY ACTION PLAN

Pray for God to give you boldness to speak the truth.

MY PERSONAL NOTES

And Action Plan

WEEK 8: CHARIOTS AFIRE

> Know ye not that they which run in a race run all, but one receiveth the prize? So run, that ye may obtain.
>
> — I CORINTHIANS 9:24

Unlike Eric Liddell, career writers are not in a 400-meter race, but in a marathon. I believe that writers have to train for the long haul and keep doing better than their previous personal best times. That's a lot of running, this marathon. Perhaps we might even feel like the messenger Pheidippides, but with better personal results.

Take heart. Laurels await.

Here are five ways I think we inspirational writers can avoid burning up our writing chariots before reaching the publishing finish line:

1. Trust God.
2. Maintain priorities.
3. Write well.
4. Encourage other writers.
5. Don't panic.

Writers require a tremendous amount of patience and wisdom as our mettle is tested from start to finish.

WEEK 8 DAILY ACTION PLAN

Pray for endurance.

MY PERSONAL NOTES

And Action Plan

WEEK 9: MAINTAIN GOOD WORKS

" And let ours also learn to maintain good works for necessary uses, that they be not unfruitful.

— TITUS 3:14

We writers all know there is life away from the writing desk. Family, friends, and faith surround us. I believe that the best writers interact well with the world around them. They are involved in the lives of the people surrounding them. They're not isolationists.

Have I been so immersed in my writing projects

that I neglected the family, friends, and people around me?

Have I forgotten that, as a novelist, I do not actually live in my own world of imaginary protagonists and invented places and time periods?

My quiet times with God in the mornings and my family obligations during the day tether me to solid reality so I don't float away into my story worlds.

I juggle multiple hats during the day. I write part time before and after school, but during school hours, I'm an educator until I finish grading those homework assignments. On weekends, we have family and church time. All these duties anchor me to the reality of serving Christ including the good works He wants me to do beyond writing and publishing my books.

I pray that I will be fruitful to the Lord (Titus 3:14).

WEEK 9 DAILY ACTION PLAN

Keep a healthy perspective on life today.

MY PERSONAL NOTES

And Action Plan

WEEK 10: AMONG WRITERS

> Rejoice with them that do rejoice, and weep with them that weep.
>
> — ROMANS 12:15

*A*re we happy for writers whose books are published while ours languish on the cutting room floor? Rejoice with them.

Do we sympathize with writers whose manuscripts are rejected by literary agents? Weep with them.

Good sportsmanship goes a long way.

The best way for me to support my author friends

is to encourage them to keep going. Regardless of whether I read the genres they write in or they read mine, I shouldn't neglect the camaraderie among writers. Birds of a feather and all that.

How do writers encourage one another? One way is to be a part of a writers' group of some kind. While there are large writers' organizations with their rules and dues, there are also smaller informal groups that communicate online and sometimes get together in person. Christian writers have fellowship with one another through those groups, share ideas, publishing, and marketing tips, and cheer one another on.

Being among other Christian writers is like going to a church social with members from all over the world. I think it's a good idea to join the conversations, get to know other writers, hear about their writing journeys, encourage others, and be encouraged as well. Iron sharpens iron (Proverbs 27:17).

I believe that as a Christian writer, there is a certain amount of calling involved. Most of us would say that we have been called to write. However, hesitation, trepidation, fear, doubt, procrastination, personal failures, and such obstacles can interrupt a writer's path to publishing. God's calling is there, but my responses can fall short due to my own human inadequacies. It's during those times of inadequacies that I need encouragement from God and from others to press on.

Writing can be a lonely job because many writers write alone with their own thoughts. It's a good thing, then, to have opportunities away from the writing desk to be among other writers who are also called to write, who understand the process of heeding God's call, as unique as is each writer's calling.

WEEK 10 DAILY ACTION PLAN:

Encourage other writers.

MY PERSONAL NOTES

And Action Plan

WEEK 11: A PLACE TO WRITE

66 And in the morning, rising up a great while before day, he went out, and departed into a solitary place, and there prayed.

— MARK 1:35

An allocated time and designated place for me to write takes me far toward my writing goals. I might require a desk and silence around me so that I can write, but I have heard of writers who could write through anything, doing their best works on the subways or while dictating to their voice recognition software or with kids running about their home office. To each his or her own.

A place to write is one thing. But a place to pray and study God's Word is even more important. If Jesus Christ, Son of God, had a definite place in which to pray, that's a lesson for me. If He sought the Father's face in the quiet of a "solitary place," then I need to consider that the still and quiet voice of God needs to cut through the noises of a busy day.

I pray all day long and anywhere, but I find that at a special place where I sit and spend time with God in His Word, He does these for me:

- Refreshes my spirit.
- Rejuvenates my soul.
- Renews my body.

After that, the rest of the day awaits.

WEEK 11 DAILY ACTION PLAN:

Spend time in God's Word.

MY PERSONAL NOTES

And Action Plan

WEEK 12: A STORY TO TELL

Being confident of this very thing, that he which hath begun a good work in you will perform it until the day of Jesus Christ.

— PHILIPPIANS 1:6

hat is your story? How much of you are woven into your writings, your manuscripts, your books?

As much as I would like to separate my writings from me, when I write out of the thoughts of my heart, there is a lot of me in what I write. Inevitably, my beliefs, my pet peeves, my wants, even my angst are entwined in my books, whether fiction or nonfiction, for the entire world to see.

For that reason, I have to be sure of what I speak, of what I write. Is my confidence in my own ability to wield a word and throw those daggers of phrases? Or is my confidence in God, who had "begun a good work" in me and who will "perform it until the day of Jesus Christ"?

Is my message my own, or is His message mine?

If God has given me a story to write, a song to sing, a poem to share, then I can be confident that He will also give me the voice and time to accomplish it.

WEEK 12 DAILY ACTION PLAN:

Be confident in Christ.

MY PERSONAL NOTES

And Action Plan

WEEK 13: BE TEACHABLE

" Call unto me, and I will answer thee, and show thee great and mighty things, which thou knowest not.

— JEREMIAH 33:3

Suppose I have my calendar all chalked up, penciled in, printed out, and somehow my plans get messed up. What do I do?

What I need to do is pray and surrender my plans and purpose to God. Perhaps some of these points might be the reasons for my scheduling failure.

- I am on the right track, but my obstacles and adversaries are many.
- My plan is not God's plan, and He is showing me the right path.
- My plan is fine, but the timing isn't right.
- My plan isn't done right, and I need to debrief, regroup, and start over.
- I am where I need to be, and such is the mountain I have to climb.
- My plan worked up to now, but it's time to factor in new dynamics and variables.

When I humble myself before the Lord and am teachable in His sight, then it's easy for me to commit the process and product to His perfect will for my writing life.

> Thy word is a lamp unto my feet, and a light unto my path.

> — PSALM 119:105

WEEK 13 DAILY ACTION PLAN:

Ask God to teach you something you didn't know.

MY PERSONAL NOTES

And Action Plan

WEEK 14: HAPPILY FLEXIBLE

66 He that handleth a matter wisely shall find good: and whoso trusteth in the Lord, happy is he.

— PROVERBS 16:20

There are things beyond human control: illnesses, deaths in the family, accidents, tornadoes, hurricanes, etc. However, we can prepare for such events, even just a little, even if it's only to prepare our own hearts and minds for it. Then there is enough flexibility for us to handle these unexpected events as they come.

When they do come, I remind myself to turn my eyes on Jesus. Focus on God. I pray, pray, pray. And then I pray some more. I study the Bible, ask God for wisdom, pay attention to sermons at church, mind the Holy Spirit when He speaks, and keep alert.

When I look at my own life thus far, I ask:

- Am I doing all that I need to do?
- Am I doing too much? Too little?
- Are my wants trumping my needs?
- Am I pursuing things that are selfish and self-serving to the detriment of my family and myself?

To be flexible, I have to be willing to let some of my plans go in favor of God's plans, that is, assuming I am sure of His plans for me. Just because a plan looks great or smells wonderful, it doesn't mean that plan comes from God. I have to handle the matter wisely, as Proverbs 16:20 reminds me.

While I cannot help but be flexible if I want to succeed, I also have to be careful that my desire to be flexible doesn't take me away from God instead of toward Him.

WEEK 14 DAILY ACTION PLAN:

Pray for godly discernment.

MY PERSONAL NOTES

And Action Plan

WEEK 15: EVERLASTING LIFE

> For God so loved the world, that he gave his only begotten Son, that whosoever believeth in him should not perish, but have everlasting life.
>
> — JOHN 3:16

Good Friday and Easter Sunday are not the only days of the year in which I think about what Jesus Christ has done for me. All year round, I rest in the assurance that:

- Jesus loves me.

- Jesus saved me.
- Jesus is always with me.

John 3:16 explains God's entire salvation plan in one verse. His plan to save us from our sins and to give us eternal life is fully explained in this verse.

- God loves me.
- God gave His only Son for me.
- I believe in His Son, Jesus.
- Therefore I won't perish.
- But have everlasting life.

If you know Jesus, rejoice. The biggest remedy of all has been provided. God sent His Son, Jesus, to save us from our sins and to give us eternal life.

WEEK 15 DAILY ACTION PLAN:

Thank God for your salvation in Christ.

MY PERSONAL NOTES

And Action Plan

WEEK 16: THANKFULNESS

" And let the peace of God rule in your
hearts, to the which also ye are called in
one body; and be ye thankful.

— COLOSSIANS 3:15

*I*t's easy to talk about having a great
attitude when everything is going well in
our writing corner. It's easy to say that our attitude
stems from our beliefs. What we believe in our
personal life will color our attitude in our professional
writing life. Inspirational writers have an added
burden of walking the talk. Nobody likes a cranky

writer of any beliefs with a bad attitude when his or her writing career tanks.

But what about our own personal walk on those days when nothing goes right?

I have had a few of those days when I can't use those 3,000 words I just wrote the day before, or worse yet, those 10,000 words I wrote the weeks before. I have had those days when nothing I wrote moved the work-in-progress forward, when it seemed like an impossible task to get the entire series written, and when I had a hard time focusing on writing due to a death in the family.

Even on those dark days, "the peace of God" should still rule in my heart, and thankfulness should still be on my mind.

Should.

But that's easy to say.

However, with God's help, by the power of the Holy Spirit, I can be clothed with the right attitude. The question is whether I believe God enough to let Him change my attitude into one of gratitude.

WEEK 16 DAILY ACTION PLAN:

Check your attitude today.

MY PERSONAL NOTES

And Action Plan

WEEK 17: JOY OF THE LORD

> Then he said unto them, Go your way, eat the fat, and drink the sweet, and send portions unto them for whom nothing is prepared: for this day is holy unto our Lord: neither be ye sorry; for the joy of the Lord is your strength.
>
> — NEHEMIAH 8:10

Should I be overjoyed even if I'm having a bad writing day? Even more so. Speaking for myself, I should be overjoyed that God is with me. If all I have is God, what more do I need?

The joy of God is my strength. I rejoice that God has given me—and all Christian writers—a gift of writing. I should patiently work on my craft, God's strength to endure encouraging me forward.

- I should rejoice when I have reached my daily word count, daily chapter quota, or whatever my goals are for writing that day, which could include editing the last chapter.
- I should rejoice even when all I have written all day are just three words. Or if I write nothing at all that day.
- Ultimately, I should rejoice in the Lord always. Again, I say rejoice!

I should be overjoyed that God has given me this amazing opportunity to do what I have always loved to do: write.

WEEK 17 DAILY ACTION PLAN:

Thank God that He is with you.

MY PERSONAL NOTES

And Action Plan

WEEK 18: DETERMINATION

> Cast not away therefore your confidence, which hath great recompence of reward. For ye have need of patience, that, after ye have done the will of God, ye might receive the promise.
>
> — HEBREWS 10:35-36

If we stop to think about it, many of us are stubborn about many things. We have opinions, pet peeves, and favorite books to read, just to name a few. What about our publishing goals?

I should be obstinate about my publishing goals if this is the career God has given to me. I should be tenaciously going toward them.

Obviously, to be doggedly persistent about a goal, I'd better be on the right track.

- I should be sure that my goals are God-approved so that I won't try to break down doors that God has closed or shut doors that He has opened. Discernment will help me determine what my goals should be.
- I should be persistent. I should press on toward the upward call. I can't shrink back.
- I should not get distracted, looking to the left or right. If I keep referring back to the goal, I won't forget what I'm writing toward.
- I should be determined to get my current manuscripts done, regardless of how many I have completed last year or last decade.

However, most of all, I should place all my confidence in Jesus, knowing that the promise of my rewards come only after I have been found faithful in patiently doing the will of God for my life.

WEEK 18 DAILY ACTION PLAN:

Determine to please God today.

MY PERSONAL NOTES

And Action Plan

WEEK 19: COUNTING COSTS

> For which of you, intending to build a tower, sitteth not down first, and counteth the cost, whether he have sufficient to finish it?
>
> — LUKE 14:28

*B*eing organized in both my personal life and my writing life will go a long way toward saving time, energy, and, yes, money.

Each hour that I fail to do what I should be doing is time wasted that cannot be reclaimed. Like the morning dew on a blade of grass, the minutes evaporate and vanish into the irrevocable past.

So, I should be organized. Pronto.

I should work on getting things in order and do them decently. As an inspirational writer, I have to get my priorities straight. I can't forget God and family:

- Set time to grow in the grace of the Lord.
- Set time for my family. Never neglect the family.
- Set time to pray, go to church, and attend Bible study.
- Set time to write.

WEEK 19 DAILY ACTION PLAN:

Pray over your checklist before executing it.

MY PERSONAL NOTES

And Action Plan

WEEK 20: COLD PLOW

The sluggard will not plow by reason of
the cold; therefore shall he beg in harvest,
and have nothing.

— PROVERBS 20:4

Setting mile markers along my writing
career, at which I stop to evaluate where I
am and where I am going, makes me flexible with the
vagaries of life. Sometimes, with new information, I
need to adjust my course, my activities, and even my
goals, if required.

Objectivity requires that I don't hinge my entire

writing career on my emotions. For example, I have a manuscript to complete within a set period of time. Whether I feel like it or not, I must want to do it. The fire in my bones burns bright. Or burns out.

When outside variables affect my productivity, for example, if editors are not available at the right time, then I should check my spirit and attitude to be sure that I respond to the speed bumps in a way that fits who I am in Christ.

As a writer, I'm inherently creative, and I write feelings into my manuscripts. Those feelings can sometimes cause subjectivity to seep into my view toward my writing career. If I don't feel like it, I don't write. If I feel great, I write. If I keep living by my emotions that way, then invariably, I will "beg in harvest, and have nothing" (Proverbs 20:4b).

WEEK 20 DAILY ACTION PLAN:

Ask God to make you productive.

MY PERSONAL NOTES

And Action Plan

WEEK 21: GIANT SLAYERS

> David said moreover, The Lord that delivered me out of the paw of the lion, and out of the paw of the bear, he will deliver me out of the hand of this Philistine. And Saul said unto David, Go, and the Lord be with thee.
>
> — I SAMUEL 17:37

*D*o you have giants you have to slay on your writing journey toward publication? Giant doubts? Giant obstacles? Giant roadblocks that are hampering your progress in meeting your writing goals or holding you back from the successes you have dreamed of?

When David fought Goliath, he had no doubt that he would slay the giant. His confidence was borne out of God's faithfulness to him in his past.

Just like David, Joshua had the same confidence to overcome his giants. He had watched God work in the lives of Moses and the Israelites as He delivered them from Egypt through the desert to the edge of the Promised Land. With Moses dead and he in charge, Joshua faced new challenges. Giants of his own.

Joshua's giants included the Jordan River, warring tribes, giant walls, the great unknown terrain ahead of him, and the sheer task of having to lead millions of people to the Promised Land, where they faced more giants. We could extend this list to include philosophical giants, emotional giants, and all the other kinds of unseen giants.

Yet, God knew what giants Joshua would face. Soon after Moses died, God gave Joshua his locker room pep talk outlined in Joshua 1:9:

- God commanded Joshua to be strong and courageous.
- God told him not to be afraid or dismayed.
- God said that He would be with Joshua whithersoever he went.

Watch out. Giants are everywhere along writing journeys. But like David and Joshua, we can overcome these obstacles by the mercy and grace of God and reach our writing and publishing goals.

WEEK 21 DAILY ACTION PLAN:

Ask God for courage.

MY PERSONAL NOTES

And Action Plan

WEEK 22: WAYFARING WRITERS

> Have not I commanded thee? Be strong and of a good courage; be not afraid, neither be thou dismayed: for the Lord thy God is with thee whithersoever thou goest.

> — JOSHUA 1:9

God is with us. He means what He says. He does what He says He'll do.

Christian writers, take heart: God is with us wherever we go.

Last week, when we discussed giants, I mentioned Joshua. This is the verse in reference. We talked about what God told Joshua He'd do for him.

This week, the same verse raises another plate of questions:

- Am I with God?
- Am I walking with Him?
- Am I going places that honor His name?
- Or am I going where my testimony will be ruined?

In writing, I usually have an idea where I want to take my story. I know the ending before I write the beginning and middle. However, it's not always so in real life. Only God knows the ending. All I know are the few steps ahead of me. God's lamp shines just enough for me to see where I need to step forward to stay safe on my writing journey.

Thy word is a lamp unto my feet, and a light unto my path.

— PSALM 119:105

WEEK 22 DAILY ACTION PLAN:

Walk with God today. Don't wander around aimlessly.

MY PERSONAL NOTES

And Action Plan

WEEK 23: CHRIST OR CIRCUMSTANCES

> But when he [Peter] saw the wind boisterous, he was afraid; and beginning to sink, he cried, saying, Lord, save me. And immediately Jesus stretched forth his hand, and caught him, and said unto him, O thou of little faith, wherefore didst thou doubt?
>
> — MATTHEW 14:30-32

As a Christian writer, I can say this: if I trust that God has called me to be a writer, then writing is for me. One way or another, I write. Come wind and high water, I have to keep the faith. But what if difficulties come?

Peter's walk was sure-footed when he kept his eyes on Christ. When he turned his eyes away from Christ onto the circumstances of that moment:

1. Peter "saw the wind boisterous."
2. He "was afraid."
3. He found himself "beginning to sink."
4. He cried out, "Lord, save me."

Peter had to realize his need for Jesus before he could see the help he required. Ever compassionate, our Lord Jesus responded instantaneously. He reached out and caught Peter.

I don't want to be guilty of this: "O thou of little faith, wherefore didst thou doubt?" My four-part action plan is thus:

1. Have faith in God through Jesus Christ.
2. Don't doubt what God has said.
3. Focus on Jesus.
4. Do the task He has assigned to me.

WEEK 23 DAILY ACTION PLAN:

Don't panic. Trust God.

MY PERSONAL NOTES

And Action Plan

WEEK 24: NEVER HUNGER, NEVER THIRST

> And Jesus said unto them, I am the bread of life: he that cometh to me shall never hunger; and he that believeth on me shall never thirst.
>
> — JOHN 6:35

Writing is hard work, but life is much harder. I thought of that when I saw a meme the other day with a photograph of a child in despair, and these words under it:

> Hardships often prepare ordinary people for extraordinary destiny.
>
> — C.S. LEWIS

As a Christian writer, I am reminded of the Prince of Peace.

Jesus Christ provides bread so we will never go hungry.

And He provides living water so we will never go thirsty.

I couldn't refuse God's offer to:

- Never hunger again.
- Never thirst again.

Do you have this assurance? Do share your hope.

Are you in despair? Hope in Jesus Christ.

WEEK 24 DAILY ACTION PLAN:

Ask God to take care of every detail in your life today.

MY PERSONAL NOTES

And Action Plan

WEEK 25: WANTING NOTHING

> My brethren, count it all joy when ye fall into divers temptations; Knowing this, that the trying of your faith worketh patience. But let patience have her perfect work, that ye may be perfect and entire, wanting nothing.
>
> — JAMES 1:2-4

As a writer, what do you do to prevent failures, if possible, and to recover from them, if necessary? Here are three things I learn when I fail:

1. Faith Loves
2. Love Hopes
3. Hope Endures

1. FAITH LOVES:

The Bible encourages us to walk by faith, not by sight. When Peter walked by faith, he walked on water. When he walked by sight, he began sinking. I pray that my faith is not puny.

> And Peter answered him and said, Lord, if it be thou, bid me come unto thee on the water. And he said, Come. And when Peter was come down out of the ship, he walked on the water, to go to Jesus. But when he saw the wind boisterous, he was afraid; and beginning to sink, he cried, saying, Lord, save me. And immediately Jesus stretched forth his hand, and caught him, and said unto him, O thou of little faith, wherefore didst thou doubt?
>
> — MATTHEW 14:28-31

2. LOVE HOPES:

If everything else fails, there is always hope in God. He never fails. It's illustrated here. The public domain King James Bible uses the word "charity," the 1611 word for "love."

> Charity suffereth long, and is kind; charity envieth not; charity vaunteth not itself, is not puffed up, Doth not behave itself unseemly, seeketh not her own, is not easily provoked, thinketh no evil; Rejoiceth not in iniquity, but rejoiceth in the truth; Beareth all things, believeth all things, hopeth all things, endureth all things.
>
> — 1 CORINTHIANS 13:4-7

3. HOPE ENDURES:

Again, using 17th century translation sure opens up etymology discussions. But the 1611 word "temptations" in the passage below means "trials." And "perfect" means "complete." We all want to be complete, wanting nothing, don't we?

> My brethren, count it all joy when ye fall

into divers temptations; Knowing this, that the trying of your faith worketh patience. But let patience have her perfect work, that ye may be perfect and entire, wanting nothing.

— JAMES 1:2-4

WEEK 25 DAILY ACTION PLAN:

Thank God for your failures.

MY PERSONAL NOTES

And Action Plan

WEEK 26: THIS WAY, THAT WAY

> For do I now persuade men, or God? or do I seek to please men? for if I yet pleased men, I should not be the servant of Christ.

— GALATIANS 1:10

*C*hristian writers, if God calls you to publish traditionally, do it. If God calls you to go indie, do it. Whatever He calls you to do, obey Him. Grace and peace to all.

I've been learning that I do not seek to please men but to please God. That is, I do not write to please an agent or a publisher, but I write to please God. My validation doesn't come from signed publishing contracts but from God.

Paul said it best in the verse above (Galatians 1:10). That is freeing for me because in the new publishing world, I am at liberty to write what I want to write, not write to get picked up by an agent or to gain a publisher's favor. Whether I publish my books traditionally or self-publish, I haven't failed either way. Nope. I'm still a writer.

The best thing I can do as a Christian writer is to trust God. If He has called me to write, He will provide for me an avenue for each of my books to be published, whether independently or traditional or a bit of both or, for that matter, neither. Those roads diverging in the publishing woods change every year as authors move from traditional publishing to self-publishing or vice versa or straddle the fence. Whether my own publishing journey is in the way I expect or not, I'll remember to give thanks to God.

Whichever path I take, I go with my eyes open:

- If traditional publishing, I need to know its limitations and benefits.
- If self-publishing, I should know the amount of labor required.
- If hybrid publishing, I would do well to try to get the best of both worlds.

WEEK 26 DAILY ACTION PLAN:

Look for the approval of God instead of the accolades of men.

MY PERSONAL NOTES

And Action Plan

WEEK 27: EXERCISED THEREBY

> Now no chastening for the present seemeth to be joyous, but grievous: nevertheless afterward it yieldeth the peaceable fruit of righteousness unto them which are exercised thereby.

> — HEBREWS 12:11

Here's my prime directive as a writer: Go write.

The more I write, the more I write. Inertia takes over, momentum impels me forward, and my muscles are "exercised thereby," to borrow a lesson from Hebrews 12:11.

Such is the same with our spiritual life.

For those of us who profess Christ as our Lord and Savior, the more we spend time studying the Bible, the more Bible we know, and the more time we want to dedicate to studying the Scripture. It builds up. We are thus "exercised thereby."

What is this "chastening" that's not "joyous, but grievous?"

Well, we know that Christians are supposed to grow up. We are not supposed to remain babies throughout our spiritual life. We are to learn, grow, mature, learn, grow, mature... until our dying day.

Supposed to, anyway.

Sadly, not all Christians grow up. Some of us remain baby Christians our entire adult lives, repeating the same mistakes over and over. Some of us are partially grown up.

Speaking for myself, I might be spiritually mature in one area but in other areas, I'm lagging behind. And yet, when I find myself taking spiritual baby steps and I fall all over my own immaturity, merciful God sweeps me up, cleans the mud off my face, bandages my grazed elbows and knees, and puts me back on the right track for a second—or maybe twentieth—chance.

However, if we do learn and grow, then we are

"exercised thereby," and we mature as a Christian, just as having exercised our writing skills, we mature as writers, albeit on a smaller scale than where our souls are concerned.

WEEK 27 DAILY ACTION PLAN:

Ask God to teach you to be spiritually mature today.

MY PERSONAL NOTES

And Action Plan

WEEK 28: FREE IN CHRIST

> If the Son therefore shall make you free, ye shall be free indeed.

> — JOHN 8:36

The Declaration of Independence of the United States of America is the human soul that yearns to break free from all bonds and chains. The human soul yearns to be:

- Free to speak.
- Free to assemble.
- Free to worship.

- Free to write.

Did you say free to write?

Yes, free to write. As a writer, that means this: I am free to write whatever, whenever, and however.

Is that so? Can I truly write anything I want even if I am a Christian?

Well, Eleanor Roosevelt wasn't the first person to say that freedom carries with it responsibility. In fact, Paul said it long before she did.

> As ye know how we exhorted and comforted and charged every one of you, as a father doth his children, That ye would walk worthy of God, who hath called you unto his kingdom and glory.
>
> — I THESSALONIANS 2:11-12

> That ye might walk worthy of the Lord unto all pleasing, being fruitful in every good work, and increasing in the knowledge of God.
>
> — COLOSSIANS 1:10

> I therefore, the prisoner of the Lord,

beseech you that ye walk worthy of the vocation wherewith ye are called.

— EPHESIANS 4:1

To me, freedom to write means the freedom to "walk worthy" of the Lord, my calling, and my vocation. It's not the freedom to self-destruct by any means and measure but to glorify God and please Him in all manner and regard. With the Holy Spirit's help, I can live up to that calling.

While I am free to write, I remind myself that freedom had a cost. Someone had to pay the price of freedom. To set souls free from the bondage of sin, God sacrificed His only Son, Jesus Christ, crucified on the cross for our sins and rose again on the third day to give us eternal life.

Once I accepted Jesus as my Lord and Savior, I am now free in Christ. To me, that is the true meaning of freedom.

WEEK 28 DAILY ACTION PLAN:

Use your freedom wisely.

MY PERSONAL NOTES

And Action Plan

WEEK 29: HIGHER CALLING

" But seek ye first the kingdom of God, and
his righteousness; and all these things shall
be added unto you.

— MATTHEW 6:33

*A*s a Christian writer, I know that God
provides for His children, but I also know
that begging for money does not become a Christian.
In fact, the Bible says Christians should be generous
enough to help the poor, feed the widows, and take
care of the helpless. That generosity doesn't come out
of nothing. It's a given that we have to have resources

in order to support a family and give to church and charity. But is that why we write? For money?

> No man can serve two masters: for either he will hate the one, and love the other; or else he will hold to the one, and despise the other. Ye cannot serve God and mammon.

> — MATTHEW 6:24

As a Christian writer, I believe that it makes sense for my writing and publishing goals to be higher than monetary purposes. Each of us has a calling, a calling we should verify. If God has called us to this vocation of writing, then He will also provide for it. If He provides for it, then I needn't worry about what I should eat or wear. God knows what I need.

> Wherefore, if God so clothe the grass of the field, which to day is, and to morrow is cast into the oven, shall he not much more clothe you, O ye of little faith? Therefore take no thought, saying, What shall we eat? or, What shall we drink? or, Wherewithal shall we be clothed? (For after all these things do the Gentiles seek:) for your heavenly Father knoweth that ye have

need of all these things. But seek ye first the kingdom of God, and his righteousness; and all these things shall be added unto you.

— MATTHEW 6:30-33

If I am not doing what I should be doing, then I need to make course corrections to get on the right track with God, where I would seek His kingdom first. How do I do that? Surrender to Him in three ways:

- Surrender my will to His will.
- Surrender my plan to His plan.
- Surrender my timing to His timing.

WEEK 29 DAILY ACTION PLAN:

Seek God first.

MY PERSONAL NOTES

And Action Plan

WEEK 30: AND YOU KNEW

" Let every man abide in the same calling
wherein he was called.

— I CORINTHIANS 7:20

*A*s a Christian writer, was there a moment in
time when you heard the sure call of God to
write?

I've been writing since I was eight years old, typing
away on an old Olivetti. When I was thirty years old, I
reflected on my life, where I had been and where I
wanted to go. Obviously, as a Christian writer, I
sought God's counsel and wisdom about my cross-

road. I don't remember being given a verse or a commission, but I do remember that I knew in my heart without a doubt that for the rest of my life, my dream job was to be a writer.

I'm still writing part time. I hope that someday I can expand it a little more when God provides me the opportunity. God and family always come first, in that order, and writing is sandwiched somewhere between grading school assignments and keeping the home.

Still, I'm writing as much as I can. My concern is to not miss the opportunities that God gives me to write more.

WEEK 30 DAILY ACTION PLAN:

Define or refine your calling.

MY PERSONAL NOTES

And Action Plan

WEEK 31: WRITE IN PEACE

> Riches profit not in the day of wrath: but righteousness delivereth from death.
>
> — PROVERBS 11:4

*I*t is true that no matter how rich you are, your riches cannot profit "in the day of wrath." Rather, the Bible admonishes us to seek something more valuable: righteousness. It can deliver us from death (Proverbs 11:4).

For a Christian, this "righteousness" is not bought or bartered because it is wrought in Christ. Too often, so-called Christians have wielded it like a bully stick, shaking it in the faces of both Christians and non-Christians alike. The truth is that righteousness in Christ yields humility and sweetness of spirit, never arrogance and pride, both of which are manifestations of a sinful heart.

As a Christian writer, I should examine my own heart. Out of the overflow of my heart, my mouth speaks.

> A good man out of the good treasure of his heart bringeth forth that which is good; and an evil man out of the evil treasure of his heart bringeth forth that which is evil: for of the abundance of the heart his mouth speaketh.
>
> — LUKE 6:45

It's important for me, as a writer, to have peace with my God. Therein is the secret to writing well: peace in your heart. When I have the peace of God in my heart, then out of that overflow is my creativity's potential realized.

WEEK 31 DAILY ACTION PLAN:

Ask God to purify your heart today.

MY PERSONAL NOTES

And Action Plan

WEEK 32: FAINT NOT

> And let us not be weary in well doing: for
> in due season we shall reap, if we faint not.
>
> — GALATIANS 6:9

Unique DNA. Unique fingerprints. Unique you. Unique me. That's the way God made us and gifted us with special talents.

As a writer called to write, I believe I should enjoy my writing life. It shouldn't be a chore. I need to enjoy it. And I do. I don't dread it. I don't make it a chore. I just enjoy writing.

Writers, what about you? What are you doing with

those gifts that God has given you? Are you serving Him? Writing for His glory? Or are you writing for your own fame and fortune, pride and prestige?

This verse reminds me that I need to write for the Lord and not for myself. This is not a declaration but a commitment of my gifts, talents, and abilities to the Lord.

> Every man's work shall be made manifest: for the day shall declare it, because it shall be revealed by fire; and the fire shall try every man's work of what sort it is.
>
> — I CORINTHIANS 3:13

WEEK 32 DAILY ACTION PLAN:

Walk in sync with God.

MY PERSONAL NOTES

And Action Plan

WEEK 33: POINT OF VIEW

66 Trust in the Lord with all thine heart; and lean not unto thine own understanding. In all thy ways acknowledge him, and he shall direct thy paths.

— PROVERBS 3:5-6

*A*s an indie writer, I couldn't help thinking about how Christian writers would approach self-publishing with its emphasis on "self," which might mortify writers who want to remain humble. Would self-publishing be an exercise in self-sufficiency, thereby negating God-sufficiency and God-dependency?

I think not.

I think that Christian writers, whether published or not yet, know to keep in mind that our successes—and failures—come from God.

Regardless of the winds that blow across the publishing bow, I would do well to keep these in mind as I skip merrily through the meadows of the publishing world:

- Trust in the Lord with all my heart on both good days and bad.
- Do not lean on my own imperfect perception of things.
- Acknowledge God at all times.
- Anticipate God to guide me through my writing career.

WEEK 33 DAILY ACTION PLAN:

Trust God every hour of today.

MY PERSONAL NOTES

And Action Plan

WEEK 34: EBENEZER

> Then Samuel took a stone, and set it between Mizpeh and Shen, and called the name of it Ebenezer, saying, Hitherto hath the Lord helped us.

— I SAMUEL 7:12

*H*ave you come a long way? Has God brought you far? Delivered you? To God be the glory.

When Samuel named the memorial stone Ebenezer, it was significant not because the stone had any value but because it was a reminder of what Samuel's God had done for the Israelites.

As a Christian writer, I have to ask myself if I make the effort to lift up my God in my writing endeavors and to give Him due credit and praise when He has delivered me through a difficult writing stretch. After all, it's not my author name that means anything, but it's the name of Jesus Christ that means eternity.

Do I pile up my own Ebenezers to remind myself of what God has done for me in my writing journey? I desire to never forget God's goodness and grace to me.

Again, to God alone be the glory.

WEEK 34 DAILY ACTION PLAN:

Write down what God has done for you today.

MY PERSONAL NOTES

And Action Plan

WEEK 35: PULSE CHECK

> And having food and raiment let us be
> therewith content.
>
> — I TIMOTHY 6:8

*P*ulse check, my writing friends. What's your attitude today?

How many times have I thought that the road to publication is difficult and the road to be an independent author quite complex?

Well, even once is too many.

Then God reminds me of things harder than writing, things like speaking to hundreds of thousands of people around the world, skydiving, surfing, singing, and so forth, all of which Nick Vujicic has done sans limbs. I can't even do a tenth of what he's done. All I am trying to do is finish my writing projects. How easy is that? Shame on me for complaining.

And what about Fanny Crosby, the hymn writer, who had been blind since infancy? Over and over, her hymns lifted the downtrodden, encouraged the weary, cheered on the saints and all the while glorifying Jesus Christ. Who am I to speak of difficulties? Again, shame on me for complaining.

WEEK 35 DAILY ACTION PLAN:

Pray that God will make your attitude more Christ-like.

MY PERSONAL NOTES

And Action Plan

WEEK 36: A JOYFUL HEART

66 A merry heart doeth good like a medicine:
but a broken spirit drieth the bones.

— PROVERBS 17:22

*A*re you a happy writer who has found
success? That is, you didn't frown your way
to a tidy net profit?

Writing is hard work. Fun, but hard work. Anyone
who says otherwise is probably not writing or
publishing.

My parents' love of literature was how I started

loving to read and write. They are very supportive of whatever I want to do in life. Their only question has always been and is still: "Are you happy?" As long as I am happy, they are fine. Great parents to have.

Yet, as Christians, we have to take it a step further. There is something more profound than happiness: joy. Strong's Concordance says that is the meaning of the word "merry" in "merry heart" (Proverbs 17:22).

Do you have a joyful heart?

My joy is borne out of my relationship with God through Jesus Christ, regardless of circumstances du jour. That is to say, in spite of the vagaries of publishing weather, my joy remains because it is secured by Christ. Writer, do you have that joy?

When I have the joy of the Lord in my heart, then there are medicinal results (Proverbs 17:22). In other words, when my heart is joyful, I become a blessing to others.

The inverse is true. When I don't have the joy of the Lord in my heart, then my spirit is broken (Proverbs 17:22).

Do you remember Ezekiel's valley of dry bones? I think that's the word picture here. My broken spirit can dry up bones. I don't want to be a curse to others, do you?

WEEK 36 DAILY ACTION PLAN:

Be a blessing to others today.

MY PERSONAL NOTES

And Action Plan

WEEK 37: I, WRITER

> For do I now persuade men, or God? or do I seek to please men? for if I yet pleased men, I should not be the servant of Christ.
>
> — GALATIANS 1:10

I write even if nobody else reads it. Called to write, nothing else has the same anodyne until I fulfill that calling. I hear it in my mind, my heart, my soul.

Write.

Write now.

To me, the most important thing is whether I am

trusting and obeying God in the way He is leading me. Therein is the rub: "the way He leads."

How do I know where the Lord is leading me in my writing career? Am I truly going where He wants me to go, or am I superimposing my own will upon His under the guise of a divine calling?

I believe that prayer and discernment are required to cut through the fog. These are some of the questions I can ask myself as I pray and seek God's will for my writing career:

- God does not contradict Himself. Is what I think I should be doing contrary to His word? Watch out!
- God's calling draws me closer to Him. Is what I am writing more in line with the spirit of the world or, worse yet, of evil, than the Spirit of God?
- God's timing is perfect. Am I pushing through closed doors and shuttered windows, so to speak?

In the end, I am happiest when I am faithful to God. I pray that I will remain faithful to Him the rest of my life. At the end of all things, this is sweet music to the faithful's ears:

" His lord said unto him, Well done, good

and faithful servant; thou hast been faithful over a few things, I will make thee ruler over many things: enter thou into the joy of thy lord.

— MATTHEW 25:23

WEEK 37 DAILY ACTION PLAN:

Verify God's calling for your writing career.

MY PERSONAL NOTES

And Action Plan

WEEK 38: LIGHT SO SHINE

> Let your light so shine before men, that they may see your good works, and glorify your Father which is in heaven.

— MATTHEW 5:16

The Fresnel lens was quite an invention. Able to give out light across choppy seas in treacherous weathers, lighthouses of olden days fitted with the Fresnel lenses prevented many sailing ships from crashing into rocks and spewing sailors into the deep.

But the lighthouses have to be lit from within. Without those fires within, those lenses could reflect only darkness. In the same way, if I am to let my light shine before people, there has to be a light in my heart to start with. For any kind of permanence, that light has to be Jesus Christ. All other lights dim in comparison.

For Christian writers, Jesus Christ is the Light of the world.

> I am come a light into the world, that whosoever believeth on me should not abide in darkness.
>
> — JOHN 12:46

The steps are clearly outlined in Matthew 5:16 in such a way that it's impossible for me to glorify God without first going through steps 1 and 2:

1. "Let your light so shine before men."
2. "They may see your good works."
3. They may "glorify your Father which is in heaven."

Am I reflecting the light of Christ to those around me? Am I doing that through good works borne out of

God's purpose and not my own design? If it is the latter, then I know that God cannot be glorified out of my sin of selfishness. Oh, I pray that all I do will reflect Christ and glorify God.

WEEK 38 DAILY ACTION PLAN:

Don't block Christ's light from shining.

MY PERSONAL NOTES

And Action Plan

WEEK 39: CHARACTER COUNTS

> Let no man despise thy youth; but be thou an example of the believers, in word, in conversation, in charity, in spirit, in faith, in purity.
>
> — I TIMOTHY 4:12

We writers often spend a lot of time developing the characters in our novels. What about our own character? Here are some things I think about:

- Am I developing godliness as I go about my writing business?
- Am I kinder today than I was yesterday?
- Am I more hardworking today than last week?
- Am I maturing in all aspects of my life as the years roll on?

Frankly, I often fall short on the above. Going through the checklist in I Timothy 4:12, I ask myself if I am an example to others in these areas?

- Word
- Conversation
- Charity
- Spirit
- Faith
- Purity

If I still fall short, as I often do, it means I'm not relying on the Holy Spirit of God to guide me through my Christian life. I repent before God, ask for forgiveness, and surrender my character to Him for repairs!

WEEK 39 DAILY ACTION PLAN:

Examine your heart today. Is it pleasing to God?

MY PERSONAL NOTES

And Action Plan

WEEK 40: A DILIGENT WRITER

> The thoughts of the diligent tend only to plenteousness; but of every one that is hasty only to want.

— PROVERBS 21:5

One of the most important disciplines a writer needs to have is diligence. Proverbs 21:5 says to me that if I am diligent, I'll have plenteousness, but if I am hasty, I'll end up with shortages. I don't want to be a needy writer.

> Go to the ant, thou sluggard; consider her

ways, and be wise: Which having no guide, overseer, or ruler, provideth her meat in the summer, and gathereth her food in the harvest.

— PROVERBS 6:6-8

Sluggard is a strong word, but the emphasis is for the contrast. The ant is a diligent creature, harvesting when there is harvest so that in the cold winter days, the ant colony might not starve. Am I that diligent? Do I work hard as though my survival depended on it?

Jesus Himself worked hard. It's a reminder for me to work too.

I must work the works of him that sent me, while it is day: the night cometh, when no man can work.

— JOHN 9:4

WEEK 40 DAILY ACTION PLAN:

Don't miss the opportunities to work.

MY PERSONAL NOTES

And Action Plan

WEEK 41: WRITING TIME

> All the ways of a man are clean in his own eyes; but the Lord weigheth the spirits.

— PROVERBS 16:2

*S*ince I am only writing part time, I'm on a time crunch whenever I get to work on my books. While I am formatting one manuscript, I'm editing another, writing a third, and researching a fourth. These tasks are confined to very limited morsels of time each week. The rest of the week, I'm teaching or cooking or driving or taking care of the family.

Hence, the question of priorities.

Writers, what are your priorities? Mine are these:

1. God
2. Family
3. Writing

I put family over writing because, like they all say, children grow up fast. Blink and they're in middle school. Blink and they're in college. However, my manuscripts are still there. I have to choose who or what matters to me. My family is more important to me than my writing career.

I have found that my writing has become richer and more vibrant because I have been there in person for my family, especially those early years of my child's life. I think I am a more informed writer today because of those years of making God and family my priority.

WEEK 41 DAILY ACTION PLAN:

Prioritize your day before it begins.

MY PERSONAL NOTES

And Action Plan

WEEK 42: SAFEKEEPING

> All the ways of a man are clean in his own eyes; but the Lord weigheth the spirits. Commit thy works unto the Lord, and thy thoughts shall be established.
>
> — PROVERBS 16:2-3

I am mindful that I need to commit my writing career to God for safekeeping.

Rather than run off on my own with a random wish list, I'm seeking God's direction in each step toward the publication of my books: what to publish, when to publish, where to publish, and how to publish.

Writers, have you placed your manuscripts on the altar of sacrifice as a sweet offering of praise unto God? I admit that I forget to do that sometimes. For me, it seems easier to hand over a completed manuscript to God. It's harder for me to place current works-in-progress or future manuscripts in the safe hands of God. Often, I'm a possessive writer who wants to own my works, forgetting to first offer them to God. Mine, all mine? Not!

When I ask, "Am I not doing all the writing here?" I am proving the case that "all the ways of a man are clean in his own eyes."

Usually, my own ideas sound great to me. What I forget is that God is God, and I am not. And when "the Lord weighs the spirits," I fall short of the glory of God.

How do I recover from this? Easy. God, the greatest outliner, writer, creator, maker of the universe and beyond, has given us two simple steps in Proverbs 16:3:

1. "Commit thy works unto the Lord."
2. "And thy thoughts shall be established."

I should be ashamed for not keeping this on top of

my daily job jar. First, I commit all my works to the Lord. Then, He will establish my thoughts. It's a promise.

WEEK 42 DAILY ACTION PLAN:

Commit all your writing projects to the Lord.

MY PERSONAL NOTES

And Action Plan

WEEK 43: PRESS ON

> I press toward the mark for the prize of the high calling of God in Christ Jesus.

— PHILIPPIANS 3:14

We all have beginnings. Roots. Origins. Some of us have been in dark miry clay, out of which God has rescued or ransomed us. Some have had relatively easy lives compared to the rest of the world. Regardless of where we come from, we all have beginnings that do color our lives and outlook. Yet, our past should not make us bitter writers.

Some of us have come a long way. Some of us are still climbing that hill. Along the journey, we meet people, share thoughts, stop to chat, and so forth. If writers snipe, gripe, and envy one another, we stall our own careers.

Every success we have comes from God. While we might have sweated blood in the fields of labor, ultimately, we Christians should be grateful to God for blessing us.

Even if we do not see the blessing we think we deserve, we should remember that God holds back some things to protect us. When the time is right, we will see the blessings. Sometimes, God chooses not to reveal to us the whys and wherefores. Who are we to demand an explanation from almighty God?

Regardless of my journey behind me, the journey ahead of me demands that I move forward and keep up with God.

> Not as though I had already attained, either were already perfect: but I follow after, if that I may apprehend that for which also I am apprehended of Christ Jesus. Brethren, I count not myself to have apprehended: but this one thing I do, forgetting those things which are behind, and reaching forth unto those things which are before, I press toward the mark

for the prize of the high calling of God in Christ Jesus.

— PHILIPPIANS 3:12-14

WEEK 43 DAILY ACTION PLAN:

Keep up with God.

MY PERSONAL NOTES

And Action Plan

WEEK 44: SEQUENCE

" He brought me up also out of an horrible
pit, out of the miry clay, and set my feet
upon a rock, and established my goings.

— PSALM 40:2

*W*riters, do you sometimes write your
chapters or scenes out of sequence?
In one of my stories, I wrote the last chapter before I
wrote the first one. In another, I wrote it inside out
from the middle. In other cases, I usually write from
chapter one straight through to the end without
jumping around.

While I might sometimes write things out of sequence in my novels, God is never out of sequence. He is a God of order, and not a God of chaos. In Psalm 40:2, the psalmist showed this sequence:

1. God brings me out of a "horrible pit" and "miry clay."
2. Then, He sets "my feet upon a rock."
3. Next, He establishes "my goings."

He rescues me, then establishes me. I see this in His salvation plan for humankind. He saves us through the blood of Jesus Christ, and then He sanctifies us continually throughout our Christian life.

The good news is that once He has done it, my path forward is secure.

WEEK 44 DAILY ACTION PLAN:

Surrender your plans to God.

MY PERSONAL NOTES

And Action Plan

WEEK 45: MANY WATERS

> The Lord on high is mightier than the noise of many waters, yea, than the mighty waves of the sea.

— PSALM 93:4

No one sails on calm waters all the time. Even the disciples had turbulent waves lashing at their little boat until Jesus calmed the stormy winds and sea.

As writers, we navigate many types of publishing oceans. Sometimes, the path is narrow and isolated.

Sometimes the route is open to eBook pirates and doldrums of low sales.

While the high seas of life might be treacherous and sometimes overwhelming, God is mightier still. Yes, He is "mightier than the noise of many waters." He is mightier than "the mighty waves of the sea."

Sometimes the winds are loud and the waves are threatening. Sometimes I become weary and lose my footing. Then I start complaining about the storm, about this, about that. That is when God has to step in to remind me that He is the Lord of the storms. In His palm is the eye of the storm. That is where I need to be.

So, stay calm in the Lord. And carry on.

WEEK 45 DAILY ACTION PLAN:

Praise God before you complain about anything.

MY PERSONAL NOTES

And Action Plan

WEEK 46: WRITE NOW

> Whereas ye know not what shall be on the morrow. For what is your life? It is even a vapour, that appeareth for a little time, and then vanisheth away.
>
> — JAMES 4:14

Are you a writer waiting for that perfect moment to write down that perfect scene percolating in your head? I won't be the first to burst that soap bubble. But here goes. There is no perfect moment on this imperfect earth to write.

There is only *now* that's given to us. Now is the time to write. After all, time stops for no one but God.

Life is full of unexpected things. For example, I didn't expect my father-in-law to get cancer and pass away fairly quickly. Even after he was diagnosed with pretty bad cancer, I still expected him to recover and go back to his life as usual. However, he worsened and never recovered on this earth. He is now in heaven with Jesus.

Instead of compiling a list of things I want to do the rest of my life, not knowing all the variables ahead, I should focus on what I must do today. While the planner in me thinks of schedules and calendars, I have to commit the future to God. Meanwhile, I can do what I need to do today. That much, I can manage. Today, I'm called to write.

So I write.

Just write. We don't know how much time we have.

> Is there not an appointed time to man upon earth? Are not his days also like the days of an hireling?
>
> — JOB 7:1

WEEK 46 DAILY ACTION PLAN:

Don't be anxious about the future. God holds it in His hands.

MY PERSONAL NOTES

And Action Plan

WEEK 47: THIS CUP

> See then that ye walk circumspectly, not as fools, but as wise, Redeeming the time, because the days are evil. Wherefore be ye not unwise, but understanding what the will of the Lord is.

> — EPHESIANS 5:15-17

I am reminded that I need to spend my time working on things that count. For Christians, working for the Lord has always proven to be the most profitable venture of all.

The caution is this: Do you know what the will of the Lord is?

Often I find myself in prayer, seeking God's will for my writing career juxtaposed with my own will, my own plan, my own desires. I have to remind myself what the Lord Jesus prayed before He was led to the crucifixion.

> And he went a little farther, and fell on his face, and prayed, saying, O my Father, if it be possible, let this cup pass from me: nevertheless not as I will, but as thou wilt.
>
> — MATTHEW 26:39

WEEK 47 DAILY ACTION PLAN:

Pray for God to reveal His will to you today.

MY PERSONAL NOTES

And Action Plan

WEEK 48: CHEERING SECTION

> Wherefore seeing we also are compassed about with so great a cloud of witnesses, let us lay aside every weight, and the sin which doth so easily beset us, and let us run with patience the race that is set before us, Looking unto Jesus the author and finisher of our faith.
>
> — HEBREWS 12:1-2A

As a writer, I need a cheering section, at least one person whose encouraging words never run out on dry writing days, someone who prays for me, sticks with me through my uphill writing journey, helps me up when I trip and fall, cheers me on to the finish line, and celebrates with me as I give God the glory.

Thank God for loyalty.

A writer's cheering section doesn't necessarily have to be family members, though that would be an affirmation indeed. Sometimes it's another writer, or a dear friend from church, or a mentor. Most importantly, if the Lord has truly called the writer to write, then He is the biggest and best cheering section.

It saddens my heart to hear that some Christian writers do not have their spouses' support in their writing careers. Marriage takes tremendous work as it is. When a husband and his wife are not supportive of each other's careers, it creates a fracture and compounds it. I pray they will find comfort and counsel in the Word of God.

What do you do for your loyal cheering section? Here is my checklist:

- Thank God for them daily.
- Pray for them as the Lord leads.
- Listen carefully to their critique.
- Repeat the above steps indefinitely.

WEEK 48 DAILY ACTION PLAN:

Pray for your supporters and readers.

MY PERSONAL NOTES

And Action Plan

WEEK 49: READY WRITER

> My heart is inditing a good matter: I speak of the things which I have made touching the king: my tongue is the pen of a ready writer.
>
> — PSALM 45:1

*A*re you a "ready writer?" Have you always loved to write? What do you write? Does it glorify God? Does it bring honor to His name?

The pastor of my church has often told the congregation that, in whatever we do, it's our duty to "give people a good opinion of Jesus."

When I do things in a hurry or out of urgency, I sometimes do it just to get it over and done with, to meet a selfish need for that moment in time. I have to remind myself to keep the bigger picture in mind, to think of things on a longer term than that minute, to defer to God's will and direction.

Since my Brownie days before I was a full-fledged Girl Scout way back when, I had to memorize Robert Baden-Powell's motto to "Be Prepared." It is even more mission critical for me as a Christian writer to be prepared spiritually.

So, am I prepared spiritually? Am I all packed and waiting? Am I ready to write whenever God calls me?

All my life's experiences since the day I was in my mother's womb until this moment in time are brought together into my readiness to obey God.

Am I a ready writer? I need to be sure.

WEEK 49 DAILY ACTION PLAN:

Be ready to write when God calls you into action.

MY PERSONAL NOTES

And Action Plan

WEEK 50: SPEEDING BULLETS

> For we walk by faith, not by sight.

— II CORINTHIANS 5:7

riters, how fast do you write?

Indie writers are often known for their prolific writing capacities and rapid production schedules. There are indies who are faster than a speeding bullet and can leap tall eBuildings in a single bound. There are indies who claim to have published over 100 books a year. Of course, one can debate about the size and length of each book, but the point is that indies are known for volume.

Meanwhile, here I am, stopping to smell the roses. Lovely day, y'all.

I'm not saying that following God is a bed of roses, that there's no striving and hard work involved. I am saying that each of us has his or her own writing, publishing, and marketing pace. Not all writers write full time, and not all writers write ten thousand words a day. Each of us needs to find his or her own equilibrium in the will of God.

Speaking for myself, I teach on weekdays during the school year. I write when I can. I could write more if I wrote for hours each day. But I do not have that luxury of time. Sometimes, I could write for hours on Saturdays and on summer breaks, perhaps, but not during the school year. I'm okay with it.

I'm at peace with the pace I have. If I try to catch up with those speeding bullets of indie publishing, I would burn out faster than an ant under a magnifying glass on a hot summer day.

So, writers, we all have our own schedules and production timelines, our own methods of sprinting or crawling to the finish line. To each his or her own.

WEEK 50 DAILY ACTION PLAN:

Don't panic.

MY PERSONAL NOTES

And Action Plan

WEEK 51: MANIFOLD GRACE

66 As every man hath received the gift, even so minister the same one to another, as good stewards of the manifold grace of God.

— I PETER 4:10

It is a wonderful thing for an author to acknowledge God as the giver of the gift of writing. A writer's desire to be a good steward working diligently on her writing projects is an inspiration to me to not grow weary when the writing life gets uphill. Pressing on because God has enabled me to write pleases God and brings joy to my writer's heart.

Our writing life can impact our family in more ways than we realize. How we view our vocation of writing will color how we manage our daily routine with that vocation woven in. As a wife and mother, I am acutely aware of what my writing career does to my family, how my publishing decisions affect the dynamics in my family both now and in the years to come.

Every day, I have to remind myself to place my writing career at the foot of the cross, at the feet of Jesus, as a sacrifice of praise, an offering of thanksgiving to God. I want God's perspective, and I accept the course corrections He leads me to make so that I may minister effectively to my family and friends and, thereby, be a good steward of the "manifold grace of God."

WEEK 51 DAILY ACTION PLAN:

Offer your writing to God as your sacrifice of praise.

MY PERSONAL NOTES

And Action Plan

WEEK 52: SWEET DENOUEMENT

> For I know the thoughts that I think toward you, saith the Lord, thoughts of peace, and not of evil, to give you an expected end.
>
> — JEREMIAH 29:11

It's my belief that all Christian writers who have a calling to write should be published, whether they publish privately for their own personal satisfaction, for their family and friends to see, or for the world at large.

If you are certain that writing is your calling, then

you have something profound to say, whether in nonfiction or fiction, and those words will be said somehow, some way, some day.

I think that the more choices readers have, the better. The better choices they have, the more informed they will be.

The more Christian writers write, the more level the playing field will be in the publishing world in terms of reading choices for our readers.

Choices, friends, are a good thing.

As a writer, it's a comfort to me that God has been with me all year long. Through days of rejoicing, days of sorrow, days of high achievements and rock bottoms, God has been with me each step of the way, guiding me, correcting me, disciplining me, and blessing me.

Is it the same with you too?

May the Lord give you a sweet denouement of success in your writing journey.

WEEK 52 DAILY ACTION PLAN:

Thank God for at least one thing every hour today.

MY PERSONAL NOTES

And Action Plan

THANK YOU FOR READING!

Thank you for reading *Writing Days*.

I hope you have been encouraged and refreshed in your walk with God.

Your review of this devotional may be helpful to others and is appreciated. Please follow the link below to find your favorite retailer where you can leave a review:

Writing Days
JanThompson.com/writing

BIBLE VERSES & ACTION PLANS

WEEK 1: A TIME TO REST

"Return unto thy rest, O my soul; for the Lord hath dealt bountifully with thee" (Psalm 116:7).

Week 1 Daily Action Plan:
Ask God to show you how to rest in Christ.

WEEK 2: AN ORDERLY ARRAY

"Let all things be done decently and in order" (I Corinthians 14:40).

Week 2 Daily Action Plan:

Get organized and stay organized.

WEEK 3: TRUSTWORTHY GOD

"Trust in the Lord with all thine heart; and lean not unto thine own understanding. In all thy ways acknowledge him, and he shall direct thy paths" (Proverbs 3:5-6).

Week 3 Daily Action Plan:

Think of God first above all else.

WEEK 4: RAISONS D'ÊTRE

"For where your treasure is, there will your heart be also" (Luke 12:34).

Week 4 Daily Action Plan:

Know your calling and don't deviate from it.

WEEK 5: TAKE HEART

"And Jesus said unto him, Go thy way; thy faith hath made thee whole. And immediately he received his sight, and followed Jesus in the way" (Mark 10:52).

Week 5 Daily Action Plan:

Ask God to increase your faith in Him.

―――――

WEEK 6: REMAIN CALM

"He maketh the storm a calm, so that the waves thereof are still" (Psalm 107:29).

Week 6 Daily Action Plan:

Pray that God will give you a calm spirit and a quiet heart.

―――――

WEEK 7: FIRE IN MY BONES

"Then I said, I will not make mention of him, nor speak any more in his name. But his word was in mine heart as a burning fire shut up in my bones, and I was weary with forbearing, and I could not stay" (Jeremiah 20:9).

Week 7 Daily Action Plan:

Pray for God to give you boldness to speak the truth.

WEEK 8: CHARIOTS AFIRE

"Know ye not that they which run in a race run all, but one receiveth the prize? So run, that ye may obtain" (I Corinthians 9:24).

Week 8 Daily Action Plan:

Pray for endurance.

WEEK 9: MAINTAIN GOOD WORKS

"And let ours also learn to maintain good works for necessary uses, that they be not unfruitful" (Titus 3:14).

Week 9 Daily Action Plan:

Keep a healthy perspective on life today.

WEEK 10: AMONG WRITERS

"Rejoice with them that do rejoice, and weep with them that weep" (Romans 12:15).

Week 10 Daily Action Plan:
Encourage other writers.

WEEK 11: A PLACE TO WRITE

"And in the morning, rising up a great while before day, he went out, and departed into a solitary place, and there prayed" (Mark 1:35).

Week 11 Daily Action Plan:
Spend time in God's Word.

WEEK 12: A STORY TO TELL

"Being confident of this very thing, that he which hath begun a good work in you will perform it until the day of Jesus Christ" (Philippians 1:6).

Week 12 Daily Action Plan:
Be confident in Christ.

WEEK 13: BE TEACHABLE

"Call unto me, and I will answer thee, and show thee great and mighty things, which thou knowest not" (Jeremiah 33:3).

Week 13 Daily Action Plan:
Ask God to teach you something you didn't know.

WEEK 14: HAPPILY FLEXIBLE

"He that handleth a matter wisely shall find good: and whoso trusteth in the Lord, happy is he" (Proverbs 16:20).

Week 14 Daily Action Plan:

Pray for godly discernment.

WEEK 15: EVERLASTING LIFE

"For God so loved the world, that he gave his only begotten Son, that whosoever believeth in him should not perish, but have everlasting life" (John 3:16).

Week 15 Daily Action Plan:

Thank God for your salvation in Christ.

WEEK 16: THANKFULNESS

"And let the peace of God rule in your hearts, to the which also ye are called in one body; and be ye thankful" (Colossians 3:15).

Week 16 Daily Action Plan:

Check your attitude today.

WEEK 17: JOY OF THE LORD

"Then he said unto them, Go your way, eat the fat, and drink the sweet, and send portions unto them for whom nothing is prepared: for this day is holy unto our Lord: neither be ye sorry; for the joy of the Lord is your strength" (Nehemiah 8:10).

Week 17 Daily Action Plan:
Thank God that He is with you.

WEEK 18: DETERMINATION

"Cast not away therefore your confidence, which hath great recompence of reward. For ye have need of patience, that, after ye have done the will of God, ye might receive the promise" (Hebrews 10:35-36).

Week 18 Daily Action Plan:
Determine to please God today.

WEEK 19: COUNTING COSTS

"For which of you, intending to build a tower, sitteth not down first, and counteth the cost, whether he have sufficient to finish it?" (Luke 14:28).

Week 19 Daily Action Plan:

Pray over your checklist before executing it.

WEEK 20: COLD PLOW

"The sluggard will not plow by reason of the cold; therefore shall he beg in harvest, and have nothing" (Proverbs 20:4).

Week 20 Daily Action Plan:

Ask God to make you productive.

WEEK 21: GIANT SLAYERS

"David said moreover, The Lord that delivered me out of the paw of the lion, and out of the paw of the bear, he will deliver me out of the hand of this Philistine.

And Saul said unto David, Go, and the Lord be with thee" (I Samuel 17:37).

Week 21 Daily Action Plan:

Ask God for courage.

WEEK 22: WAYFARING WRITERS

"Have not I commanded thee? Be strong and of a good courage; be not afraid, neither be thou dismayed: for the Lord thy God is with thee whithersoever thou goest" (Joshua 1:9).

Week 22 Daily Action Plan:

Walk with God today. Don't wander around aimlessly.

WEEK 23: CHRIST OR CIRCUMSTANCES

"But when he [Peter] saw the wind boisterous, he was afraid; and beginning to sink, he cried, saying, Lord, save me. And immediately Jesus stretched forth his hand, and caught him, and said unto him, O thou of little faith, wherefore didst thou doubt?" (Matthew 14:30-32).

Week 23 Daily Action Plan:

Don't panic. Trust God.

WEEK 24: NEVER HUNGER, NEVER THIRST

"And Jesus said unto them, I am the bread of life: he that cometh to me shall never hunger; and he that believeth on me shall never thirst" (John 6:35).

Week 24 Daily Action Plan:

Ask God to take care of every detail in your life today.

WEEK 25: WANTING NOTHING

"My brethren, count it all joy when ye fall into divers temptations; Knowing this, that the trying of your faith worketh patience. But let patience have her perfect work, that ye may be perfect and entire, wanting nothing" (James 1:2-4).

Week 25 Daily Action Plan:

Thank God for your failures.

WEEK 26: THIS WAY, THAT WAY

"For do I now persuade men, or God? or do I seek to please men? for if I yet pleased men, I should not be the servant of Christ" (Galatians 1:10).

Week 26 Daily Action Plan:

Look for the approval of God instead of the accolades of men.

WEEK 27: EXERCISED THEREBY

"Now no chastening for the present seemeth to be joyous, but grievous: nevertheless afterward it yieldeth the peaceable fruit of righteousness unto them which are exercised thereby" (Hebrews 12:11).

Week 27 Daily Action Plan:

Ask God to teach you to be spiritually mature today.

WEEK 28: FREE IN CHRIST

"If the Son therefore shall make you free, ye shall be free indeed" (John 8:36).

Week 28 Daily Action Plan:
Use your freedom wisely.

WEEK 29: HIGHER CALLING

"But seek ye first the kingdom of God, and his right-eousness; and all these things shall be added unto you" (Matthew 6:33).

Week 29 Daily Action Plan:
Seek God first.

WEEK 30: AND YOU KNEW

"Let every man abide in the same calling wherein he was called" (I Corinthians 7:20).

Week 30 Daily Action Plan:

Define or refine your calling.

WEEK 31: WRITE IN PEACE

"Riches profit not in the day of wrath: but righteousness delivereth from death" (Proverbs 11:4).

Week 31 Daily Action Plan:

Ask God to purify your heart today.

WEEK 32: FAINT NOT

"And let us not be weary in well doing: for in due season we shall reap, if we faint not" (Galatians 6:9).

Week 32 Daily Action Plan:

Walk in sync with God.

WEEK 33: POINT OF VIEW

"Trust in the Lord with all thine heart; and lean not unto thine own understanding. In all thy ways acknowledge him, and he shall direct thy paths" (Proverbs 3:5-6).

Week 33 Daily Action Plan:
Trust God every hour of today.

WEEK 34: EBENEZER

"Then Samuel took a stone, and set it between Mizpeh and Shen, and called the name of it Ebenezer, saying, Hitherto hath the Lord helped us" (I Samuel 7:12).

Week 34 Daily Action Plan:
Write down what God has done for you today.

WEEK 35: PULSE CHECK

"And having food and raiment let us be therewith content" (I Timothy 6:8).

Week 35 Daily Action Plan:

Pray that God will make your attitude more Christ-like.

WEEK 36: A JOYFUL HEART

"A merry heart doeth good like a medicine: but a broken spirit drieth the bones" (Proverbs 17:22).

Week 36 Daily Action Plan:

Be a blessing to others today.

WEEK 37: I, WRITER

"For do I now persuade men, or God? or do I seek to please men? for if I yet pleased men, I should not be the servant of Christ" (Galatians 1:10).

Week 37 Daily Action Plan:

Verify God's calling for your writing career.

WEEK 38: LIGHT SO SHINE

"Let your light so shine before men, that they may see your good works, and glorify your Father which is in heaven" (Matthew 5:16).

Week 38 Daily Action Plan:

Don't block Christ's light from shining.

WEEK 39: CHARACTER COUNTS

"Let no man despise thy youth; but be thou an example of the believers, in word, in conversation, in charity, in spirit, in faith, in purity" (I Timothy 4:12).

Week 39 Daily Action Plan:

Examine your heart today. Is it pleasing to God?

WEEK 40: A DILIGENT WRITER

"The thoughts of the diligent tend only to plenteousness; but of every one that is hasty only to want" (Proverbs 21:5).

Week 40 Daily Action Plan:

Don't miss the opportunities to work.

WEEK 41: WRITING TIME

"All the ways of a man are clean in his own eyes; but the Lord weigheth the spirits" (Proverbs 16:2).

Week 41 Daily Action Plan:

Prioritize your day before it begins.

WEEK 42: SAFEKEEPING

"All the ways of a man are clean in his own eyes; but the Lord weigheth the spirits. Commit thy works unto the Lord, and thy thoughts shall be established" (Proverbs 16:2-3).

Week 42 Daily Action Plan:

Commit all your writing projects to the Lord.

WEEK 43: PRESS ON

"I press toward the mark for the prize of the high calling of God in Christ Jesus" (Philippians 3:14).

Week 43 Daily Action Plan:
Keep up with God.

WEEK 44: SEQUENCE

"He brought me up also out of an horrible pit, out of the miry clay, and set my feet upon a rock, and established my goings" (Psalm 40:2).

Week 44 Daily Action Plan:
Surrender your plans to God.

WEEK 45: MANY WATERS

"The Lord on high is mightier than the noise of many waters, yea, than the mighty waves of the sea" (Psalm 93:4).

Week 45 Daily Action Plan:

Praise God before you complain about anything.

WEEK 46: WRITE NOW

"Whereas ye know not what shall be on the morrow. For what is your life? It is even a vapour, that appeareth for a little time, and then vanisheth away" (James 4:14).

Week 46 Daily Action Plan:

Don't be anxious about the future. God holds it in His hands.

WEEK 47: THIS CUP

"See then that ye walk circumspectly, not as fools, but as wise, Redeeming the time, because the days are evil. Wherefore be ye not unwise, but understanding what the will of the Lord is" (Ephesians 5:15-17).

Week 47 Daily Action Plan:

Pray for God to reveal His will to you today.

WEEK 48: CHEERING SECTION

"Wherefore seeing we also are compassed about with so great a cloud of witnesses, let us lay aside every weight, and the sin which doth so easily beset us, and let us run with patience the race that is set before us, Looking unto Jesus the author and finisher of our faith" (Hebrews 12:1-2a).

Week 48 Daily Action Plan:

Pray for your supporters and readers.

WEEK 49: READY WRITER

"My heart is inditing a good matter: I speak of the things which I have made touching the king: my tongue is the pen of a ready writer" (Psalm 45:1).

Week 49 Daily Action Plan:

Be ready to write when God calls you into action.

WEEK 50: SPEEDING BULLETS

"For we walk by faith, not by sight" (II Corinthians 5:7).

Week 50 Daily Action Plan:
Don't panic.

WEEK 51: MANIFOLD GRACE

"As every man hath received the gift, even so minister the same one to another, as good stewards of the manifold grace of God" (I Peter 4:10).

Week 51 Daily Action Plan:
Offer your writing to God as your sacrifice of praise.

WEEK 52: SWEET DENOUEMENT

"For I know the thoughts that I think toward you, saith the Lord, thoughts of peace, and not of evil, to give you an expected end" (Jeremiah 29:11).

Week 52 Daily Action Plan:

Thank God for at least one thing every hour today.

ACKNOWLEDGMENTS

First of all, I thank my Lord and Savior Jesus Christ for giving me this wonderful writing adventure. Everything that I have learned and recorded here in *Writing Days* is what I have learned from God.

Secondly, I am eternally grateful to God for my dear husband and dear son, both of whom have been super supportive of my writing career. It was my husband who first told me to self-publish in 2011. Three years later, I finally listened. You're the man, my love.

Thirdly, I must thank my parents and brothers, all of whom have been and are still readers. My parents created a home environment in which books were always around, from the first novel I read, *Robin Hood*, to all sorts of contemporary fiction for young people such as *Famous Five, Secret Seven, Hardy Boys,* and *Nancy Drew,* and classics such as books by Charles Dickens, Robert Louis Stevenson, and Mark Twain.

From my parents, I learned the love of writing. To this day I am writing because long ago, when I was little, my parents let me write and "publish" little handwritten stories in flip books.

After I accepted Jesus Christ as my Lord and Savior back in university, I soon found that my most favorite book in the whole world is the Bible. Nothing I ever write will ever come close to God's masterpiece literature. To God be the glory!

In Christ,
Jan Thompson
August 2014

SUBSCRIBE TO JAN THOMPSON'S MAILING LIST

Are you on *USA Today* bestselling author Jan Thompson's mailing list? Get book release news, sales and special deals, promotional notifications, and behind-the-scene-information about her clean and wholesome contemporary Christian romance, romantic suspense, and suspense thriller series.

Keep up with Jan as she writes more books for you to enjoy.

Subscribe to Jan's Mailing List:
JanThompson.com/newsletter

BOOKS BY JAN THOMPSON

CONTEMPORARY CHRISTIAN ROMANCE & ROMANTIC WOMEN'S FICTION

Savannah Sweethearts (11 Books)
JanThompson.com/savannah

Vacation Sweethearts (5 Books)
JanThompson.com/vacation

Seaside Chapel (9-12 Books)
JanThompson.com/seaside

CHRISTIAN ROMANTIC SUSPENSE & INSPIRATIONAL ROMANTIC THRILLERS

Protector Sweethearts (6 Books)
JanThompson.com/protector

Suspense Sweethearts Collection (Box Set)
JanThompson.com/suspense

Binary Hackers (3 Books)
JanThompson.com/binary

SAVANNAH SWEETHEARTS (CONTEMPORARY CHRISTIAN ROMANCE)

- Prequel: Ask You Later
- Book 1: Know You More
- Book 2: Tell You Soon (Romance with Suspense)
- Book 3: Draw You Near
- Book 4: Cherish You So
- Book 5: Walk You There
- Book 6: Love You Always (Romance with Suspense)
- Book 7: Kiss You Now
- Book 8: Find You Again
- Book 9: Wish You Joy (Christmas Romance)
- Book 10: Call You Home

Meet a group of multiethnic churchgoing Christians who love the Lord, work hard in their careers, and seek God's will for their love lives. Against a backdrop of ocean, sand, and sun, these inspirational romances showcase aspects of the human need for God and for one another.

Have some tea, settle on a comfortable reading chair, and enjoy these sweet celebrations of faith, hope, and love in Jesus Christ.

More about Savannah Sweethearts:
JanThompson.com/savannah

VACATION SWEETHEARTS (CONTEMPORARY CHRISTIAN ROMANCE)

- Book 1: Smile for Me
- Book 2: Reach for Me (Romance with Suspense)
- Book 3: Wait for Me (Romance with Suspense)
- Book 4: Look for Me (Romance with Suspense)
- Book 5: Cheer for Me

Travel with our friends from Savannah, Georgia, to the coast and to the mountains. Cheer them on as they celebrate the immeasurable grace and undeserved mercy of God through Jesus Christ.

The Vacation Sweethearts novels are a spin-off of Jan's Savannah Sweethearts series, and fans will recognize familiar faces from Riverside Chapel, a church in the coastal city of Savannah, Georgia.

In fact, we might even visit the beach town of Tybee Island from time to time to visit old friends and beloved families...

The collection begins with *Smile for Me,* the story of Byron Moss and Tina MacFarland, spending their summer on the Caribbean islands of the Bahamas where the water is blue and hearts are warm…

More about Vacation Sweethearts:
JanThompson.com/vacation

SEASIDE CHAPEL (CONTEMPORARY CHRISTIAN ROMANCE & ROMANTIC WOMEN'S FICTION)

- Book 1: Share with Me
- Book 2: Step with Me
- Book 3: Sing with Me
- (More Books to Come)

The novels of Seaside Chapel blend women's fiction with contemporary Christian romance to celebrate the grace of God and hope in Jesus Christ.

Visit Jan's favorite beach town of St. Simon's Island, Georgia, where our friends live and attend Seaside Chapel, a little church by the sea known for its beach weddings and fair shares of love and life.

As these Christians grow in their knowledge and understanding of God, they are tested in their spiritual maturity, their relationships with others, and their love lives. Share their heartaches and healing, and cheer them on as they celebrate faith, family, friends, and yes, happily-ever-afters.

The Seaside Chapel novels are all about life by the Atlantic Ocean, which in essence, is not much different from life in landlocked cities. Inherently, the human nature is such that we have in our hearts a need for the Lord, for His salvation, sustenance, and sanctification.

More about Seaside Chapel:
JanThompson.com/seaside

PROTECTOR SWEETHEARTS (CHRISTIAN ROMANTIC SUSPENSE)

- Book 1: Once a Thief
- Book 2: Once a Hero
- Book 3: Once a Spy
- (More Books to Come)

Protector Sweethearts is a spinoff of Savannah Sweethearts. This Christian Romantic Suspense series begins with *Once a Thief*, Private Investigator Helen Hu's story. Helen makes cameo appearances in *Tell You Soon* (Savannah Sweethearts Book 2) and *Step with Me* (Seaside Chapel Book 2). Helen is petite and feisty, and wears 5-inch heels. And then there's Mama Hu, the one with all those secrets causing commotions...

More about Protector Sweethearts:
JanThompson.com/protector

BINARY HACKERS (CHRISTIAN TECHNO THRILLERS WITH ROMANCE)

- Book 1: Zero Sum
- Book 2: Zero Day
- Book 3: Zero Base
- (More Books to Come)

An inspirational Christian romantic thriller series, Binary Hackers features the employees of Binary Systems, a computer security company in Atlanta, Georgia. The Binary Hackers series is a prelude to an upcoming cyber thriller series featuring Cayson's cousin. Stay tuned.

Meanwhile, Binary Hackers is set in the same story world as Jan's other books, and characters from the other series may make cameo appearances in Binary Hackers.

———————

More about Binary Hackers:
JanThompson.com/binary

ABOUT JAN THOMPSON

USA Today bestselling author Jan Thompson writes clean and wholesome contemporary Christian romance with elements of women's fiction, Christian romantic suspense with an air of mystery, and inspirational international thrillers with threads of sweet Christian romance.

Raised on a tropical island in the eastern hemisphere, Jan now lives in the western hemisphere. Her international background gives her a unique multicultural and multiracial perspective in her writing.

Jan's books are for readers who love inspiring stories of faith, hope, and love in Jesus Christ.

Jan's life verse is John 3:16.

Find out more about Jan Thompson:
JanThompson.com

For God so loved the world,
that He gave His only begotten Son,
that whosoever believeth in Him should not perish,
but have everlasting life.
—John 3:16

www.ingramcontent.com/pod-product-compliance
Lightning Source LLC
LaVergne TN
LVHW011323080426
835513LV00006B/177